The Essence Of Trading Psychology

(In One Skill)

By
Yvan Byeajee

I dedicate this book to all the new and struggling traders out there. I hope you find in it a source of inspiration and motivation to help you develop into the kind of person you need to become, in order to build the trading career you want and deserve.

INTRODUCTION

Picture this:

•   You are right in the middle of a profitable trade, and you are worried about giving back some precious unrealized gains.
•   You are stressing about the nasty drawdown you are currently in and you want that particular trade to work so that you can feel whole again.
•   You feel anxious about the money you don't have and need.
•   You think about the bills, the mortgage, the things you could afford if only you could return consistent results out of your trading operations.
•   You imagine your wife, family, friends and you worry about how they may perceive you. You want them to think that you are getting somewhere with this crazy dream of trading for a living.

Is that a common thing for you? I know what it feels like. Trying to create consistency in trading, even more so a life worth living, when overwhelmed by those states of mind is a tough battle.

For a very long time, I have experienced these states and the range of afflictive thoughts and emotions that characterize them. As a result, 5 years into trading and still I wasn't able to engineer consistency in my results.

One day, almost by mistake, I began realizing that I was, in essence, held hostage by my own thinking. All that time, I was stuck in a cage that is wide open, and I never knew there was an alternative to that.

At times, when we are most captured by fear, we are

forced into reacting blindly to new possibilities. We feel boxed in these feelings which give rise to rigid states of resistance. Hence, we often hear pieces of advice such as: *"when you trade, let your emotions at the front door"*, or *"control your emotions."* The reality, however, is far from being that simple and such advice aren't always sound.

Thoughts and emotions are part and parcel of our human experience. We can never part ways with them, but we can definitely find a way to work with them. So my suggestion is that we have to learn to use our brain in a way that engenders less resistance and better psychological satisfaction. With practice, we can learn this! It is possible to choose to respond from our higher, rational mind rather than being bossed around by our primitive mind. It just requires that we gain awareness that some of our beliefs, values, and therefore, thoughts and emotions are skillful while others are not.

Trading can be a very enjoyable experience, we just need to bring into it this quality of wise discernment. In Zen Mind, Beginner's mind, Suzuki Roshi really captured the right attitude to adopt with this quote: *"Leave your front door and back door open. Let thoughts come and go. Just don't serve them tea."*

This is a very powerful analogy to explain the kind of awareness that is needed to make it as a consistently profitable trader. In other words, we are not pushing or fighting anything. We are merely observing and "letting be."

Yvan

ABOUT THE AUTHOR

My name is Yvan Byeajee and I am the creator of Trading Composure, a blog where I share the many lessons I learned about trading, habits, beliefs, behavior, mindfulness, success, happiness, motivation,… all of which are paramount if trading for a living is something you're interested in.

I started my trading journey in 2007. Over the course of the following 5 years or so, I went through significant drawdowns – both financial and emotional. My repeated failures in the markets pushed me to question my role in the kind of results I was engineering for myself month after month, year after year.

Through this mere act of reflection and self-analysis came a whole new paradigm. Said this way, it might seem like it was smooth sailing from there – it wasn't! But slowly (and eventually), I started to become more and more consistent. 2013 was my first profitable year as a trader. That is the year where I also came in 2nd in a live trading competition.

I started Trading Composure to share the lessons failure and hardship taught me, and today I help people change their trading results through my writings.

Thank you for purchasing this book. I hope you find within it concrete answers to your struggles in the markets. *The Essence Of Trading Psychology In One Skill* is a reflection on your own potential for greatness. This means that you can raise the bar on your own limitations if you dare to do so – and I sincerely hope you do!

CONTENTS

Important note:

Reading this book and putting it aside will not make you a consistently profitable trader. Knowing something, however commendable, is not enough. We must apply! Trading for a living cannot happen if you do not change some things you do daily. So I trust that you will put the information presented in this book to good use.

1. IDENTIFYING THE PROBLEM

"A mind that clings is a mind that suffers."

Let's cut to the chase! The root of all of our problems as traders is found in our inability to detach ourselves from our story of survival. This is not an opinion, it's a fact. I firstly realized this in the laboratory of my own life as I failed, in a rather epic way, over and over again throughout the years. And I also observed it in the dozen traders I have coached and watched.

Can it really be that simple?

Yes! But to better conceptualize this answer, picture a lion in a savannah. Perhaps it's sitting in a bush and using its sharp eyes to search for food. Perhaps it has already found its prey and it's stalking it. In any case, the animal lives totally in the moment, completely focused on its current move.

Imagine for a second if this dialogue went through its mind:

- *"Why does it have to be so hot down here?"*
- *"What do the other lions think of me?"*
- *"Will I be able to catch that prey? I missed one last time and I went hungry for days."*
- *"What if I don't catch it? What's going to happen? Oh, I'm so hungry, I need this!"*

And so on.

Just let this picture settle in your mind for a moment.

Now, what do you think we do as traders?

You see, it all boils down to what is going on in our minds. Our constant attachment to certain erroneous beliefs, grandiose expectations, unresolved cravings, is what manufactures our trading results.

You might have…
- a proven edge,
- an efficient risk and money management technique,
- enough trading capital at your disposal to give you a fair chance,
- the best trading software at your disposal,
- a reliable broker with great commissions…

… but regardless of those advantages, if you are still engineering mediocrity for yourself, then some deep changes in the way you think need to be considered.

Day after day, your state of mind determines your ability to abide by your rules and act consistently in the markets. And, if you are unaware of your inner process of thinking, thoughts of an uncertain future and memories of a painful past will manufacture anxiety, stress, doubts, and self-criticisms in the present, and those will dictate behavior.

And if you think that willpower will help you engineer an optimal state of mind every day and abide by your rules, think again! Willpower is a wasting asset. Like a battery, it depletes over time and needs to be recharged. Hence, if you can't find a way to cope reliably, day after day, with this voice inside your head that is always worrying, complaining, and voicing its opinion, trading for a living will not be a viable option for you despite all the will power in the world.

"When you over-think things, you end up creating problems where they just don't exist."

In its essence, trading is just a game of applying a model to the letter. Said this way, it surely seems simple. But, simple doesn't mean easy! This is especially true when one trades for a living. And, as any real trader who does so will attest, this endeavor is a battle that is difficult to win.

Unless you have a 100 million dollar account, the pressure – to perform, to sustain a living, to pay the bills – if left unmanaged is precisely what will affect your behavior in the markets.

As humans, we have sophisticated brains. We can solve

problems; we can reason, create philosophy, science, art, etc.. So we definitely have more abilities and lots more going on than a lion.

But, possessing a human mind is a two-edged sword. These more sophisticated brains of ours are the reason why we are on top of the evolutionary chain, but they are also the cause of all the problems that we have. With their never-ending stream of thoughts, feelings, and impulses, very often they help us achieve precisely the opposite of what we desire in life.

If we are ever to find a solution to a problem, we have to identify the problem in the first place, wouldn't you agree? And, identifying the root of our patterns of problem behaviors, in or out of the markets, comes through a simple understanding: the mind has a propensity to cling to what is pleasant or common, and repudiate what is not. Hence, if we want different results, we have to change the way we respond to this call for behavior – we have to learn to relax this mechanism.

This is at the base of every trading psychology books out there, however complex words and esoteric terms they contain. It all boils down to this very important truth about the mind.

Throughout this book, I am going to discuss how and why this clinging happens. And as we'll see, this isn't serving us well, so I'll show you a simple way to discontinue, or largely reduce this automatic process.

Behind the human brain's complexity, lies a rather primitive way of operating. Its basic function is survival, hence, it naturally wants to prevent us from repeating painful experiences. It deduces that it has to hold on to survive. In doing so, by its logic, it is steering us away from danger.

But not so fast!

You see, this was very useful thousands of years ago, but today, the world has changed, and with it the quality of our lives.

Men have been on Earth for millions of years. But only in the last few hundred years has science made major advances – notably in medicine and technology. Statistically, we live in the safest time in history, and the average human life expectancy has expanded.

Collectively, we have improved our knowledge of the unknown and explored the boundaries of our limitations. We, now, have a certain degree of control over our environment, and what was once considered dangerous isn't so much anymore.

Yet, in the midst of all that progress, our brain is still lagging in some respect. It has definitely evolved in many ways, but its basic survival-based functions haven't.

The changes we, humans, went through collectively is glaring. But changes always happen on an individual level first, and if we want to become a generation of traders, advanced not merely in terms of knowledge but emotional fortitude, it's important that we learn to relax this process of clinging to what is known and comfortable.

"Nothing is permanent, except change!"

Empirically, we know how to improve the quality of our human experiences. We know that it involves stepping outside of our comfort zone and letting go of things that don't serve us well – whatever they are.

We know how to maximize desirable emotions like happiness, contentment, and how to minimize painful ones like sadness, despair, etc. We know how to do this as a matter of common sense, but the reality is that common sense is not that common.

There is a big difference between knowing something on an intellectual level and actually doing it in practice. For instance, cutting your losses and letting your winners run, are acts that are known to provide not only better results but also better psychological satisfaction. Yet, why do we find it hard to do?

Simply put, the mind's goal is to steer us away from danger. And sometimes it gets carried away, placing undue limitations on our behavior. As traders, we have to learn to take a step back from this process!

A mind that is stuck in its limiting patterns is a mind that refuses to change and to let go. My argument is that we have to learn the process of accepting and allowing change to happen in order to move beyond our limitations and step closer towards our goals.

If you haven't learned to transcend your instinctual survival-based response that impedes on your capacity to adhere to your trading methodology, chances are that you are not very consistent in your behavior, and hence, your results.

In order to succeed at the *seemingly* esoteric art of trading for a living, you have to relinquish your attachment to many unproductive habit patterns, fixed beliefs, and expectations. Regardless of how unproductive or dysfunctional these are, they came about to support this whole instinctual process of survival. So your goal is not to push them away or even punish yourself for having them. Your goal is to accept and observe yourself without feeling identical to your internal dialogue, thus relaxing that whole process of action and reaction. We'll dig deeper into that.

"Real strength is in letting go."

In practical terms, detachment means surrendering – from this insistent grip we tend to exert on beliefs, habits, visions, ideas, and expectations that don't serve us well. So we can clearly see how important a skill it is in trading – let alone in life. Yet, the resistance most traders feel to this idea is unprecedented.

For instance:

• We tend to hold too many expectations for ourselves. We stress because we want the markets to be a certain way so that the outcomes of our trades fit the box-shaped vision we have for them. When things inevitably don't go that way, we melt into grief, anger, frustration, and other limiting states of the mind.

• We cling to the pain of previous losses. We get irritated with our losses because they make us feel like losers. But, they also tap into the accumulated painful experiences we have had as a result of prior losses.

• We cling to past and future, and we repudiate the present. This is what goes on in our heads:

o   *"What if this trade I'm putting on turns out to be a loser."*

o   *"I can't enter here even though there's a signal. My last trade was a loser, this one is a sure loser too."*

o   *"I know the stock is going to rebound, I'm going to keep the trade on and ignore my stop loss."*

As a result, we become prisoners of helplessness, hopelessness, despair, fear, anxiety, stress, trivial concerns, quiet desperation, which are the distinctive features of the unprofitable trader.

• We over-identify too much with our fears. The root of our problems as traders is fear — of not having enough, of not being able to — and the root of fear is the clinging to how we want things to be.

• We focus too much on money and the vast riches trading can offer us. To various degrees, stress, fears of missing out, worries around losing, disappointments, and more, are all born of the obsession we have over money – or the reward. We don't always notice this, but it's true.

• We can't accept uncertainty. Security and certainty are the results of rigid attachment to that which is known, and we desperately try to create those where they just don't – and can't – exist. This engineers psychological resistance and makes trading unfruitful and exasperating.

That is a brief outline of what I'll be discussing in this book, but as you can see, it is hard to overstate the case for detachment. It is an essential skill that can turn you into a better trader – and it's a teachable one!

Change, however, doesn't happen with a snap of one's fingers. Detachment is a process. It's an organic cycle that needs to be cultivated. You have to know when to apply it, and how. And almost always, your ego – the you whose main concerned is survival – is going to try to stop you from doing so, since it so dearly believes that you have to hold on to survive.

In this brief but comprehensive book, we'll look at how detachment works. We'll also look at how you can develop and practice the skill. Everything you read here, from an empirical stance, doesn't only apply to trading. You can extrapolate it to other areas of your life.

"A real teacher is not a giver of truth; he is a guide, a pointer to the truth that each student must find for himself."

Before closing this first chapter, please note that when talking about detachment, I am using the term in a broader sense, which can imply acceptance and letting go. Therefore, I will substitute the word 'detachment' with 'acceptance' or 'letting go' where applicable and appropriate.

Also, I feel I need to clarify something. I grant it to you, detachment isn't appropriate for everything, nor is it practical. So, as you test things out in the laboratory of your own life, finding the right balance is crucial. Since detachment is a deeply personal choice, you are going to have to be your own teacher and guide. I can only discuss with you what has worked for me and show you the path. However, you'll have to walk that path yourself. This is your journey!

2. THE RIGHT TOOL FOR THE JOB

"If you use a hammer to drill a hole, you're going to have a hard time building anything."

Before we plunge into the esoteric, let's briefly discuss methodology – by which I mean your set of rules that define your market edge and risk parameters. Since this is the basic "tool" you need to navigate the markets, it is important that we see what constitutes a "good" methodology.

Early in my trading career, I took pride in predicting accurately where markets were headed at any given moment. My ego was so heavily involved in the process that whenever I was proven wrong in my assumptions, I would feel hurt and betrayed. If this didn't prompt me to revenge trade, I would just try to hold onto my positions until the markets would satisfy my ego and make me whole again – by making me right. Useless to say this rarely happened!

By holding my grounds and by not being flexible, I would place myself in catastrophic positions. So, as I sit back and reflect on my journey as a trader, where I was and where I am today, I can clearly point out those things that I didn't get right at the time.

One of the fundamental lessons that I've learned and come to accept is that control in the markets is an illusion. I know this as a matter of personal experience born of observation through the 4300+ trades I have placed since the beginning of my career.

"For the trained mind, uncertainty equals opportunity."

Markets are deterministic chaos processes – there is a long chain of variables (some of them random and some not) that have influenced the reality of their current condition. The markets achieve aggregate stability when people have variable time horizons and expectations for their investments. In contrast, a speculative bubble is formed when many people share the same expectations, imitating each other's decisions to buy, and a market crash occurs when they all "rush for the exit" at the same time. This is also often referred to as causation, or causality, but with a dash of "noise", or randomness because people are not always rational.

Markets are fractal, so this deterministic chaos behavior

starts incrementally small, with up or down ticks, and progresses to higher time-frames, just like a domino effect. Said this way, predicting surely seem like an easy game, but in practice one can only notice that it isn't so. Price movements (especially short-term) can be extremely difficult to predict because of the randomness component, hence, trade outcomes often bear no immediate relationship to one another.

There is a constant battle happening between momentums of aversion, fear, greed, optimism, pessimism… and we can't know for sure which one is going to prevail at any given moment, thus affecting a tick and the subsequent ones, scaling the higher time-frames.

If there was a way to gain perfect knowledge of every parameter that might cause a specific market to move in a certain way, and if we had control over these parameters, we would be able to eliminate that randomness component, making the markets pretty much predictable 100% of the time. We would create certainty.

The problem is that price reflects the behavior of millions of people interacting within a specific market, and we can't possibly get into each and everyone's head to see what is motivating their behavior in any given moment. And now, there are even computer software that buy and sell based on how they are programmed to perceive events and circumstances. So as you see, it's a difficult issue. Of course, we can make informed decisions based on analyzes and news, but these only tell us what is likely to happen, never what will happen with absolute certainty.

"Trading effectively is about assessing probabilities, not certainties."

So, rather than wasting time (or losing sleep) over things that we have no power over, what we can (and should) focus on is assessing probabilities instead of certainties. We should also focus on finding asymmetric opportunities and defining our risk prior to entry because in the end, those are the only things we can control.

The deterministic aspect of the markets allows us to go back and look at the past to see what has happened when certain conditions were met, and what the ensuing results were. Based on the readings we get through statistical studies of those conditions, we can devise a methodology to take advantage of that. If there is a reliable reading, then it's fairly reasonable to assume that, through extrapolation into the future, the results should come close to that expected value over enough number of trades.

Let's take a quick example. Suppose I give you a weighted coin, and I ask you to flip it. We know based on the law of large numbers that if you keep flipping, the coin will end on the weighted side more often than not. Let's assume in this case that you know (statistically) that 70% of the time, it will end on the weighted side. So you just have to keep flipping the coin to see that expected value eventuate.

In trading, that weighed coin is your objectively defined "edge." As you keep trading (insofar as you flawlessly adhere to your methodology that takes advantage of that edge), your results will take care of themselves through the magic of the law of large numbers – which states that if you create enough number of trade occurrences, by default you increase your probability of profit.

In my opinion, that is the least stressful way to go

about trading. There is no place for subjectivity here because the accumulated evidence that validates your trading opportunities are objectively defined with a set of "either-or" rules. For instance, either price broke the high of that 30 minutes opening range, or it didn't. Either price breaks support, or it doesn't... you get the point.

"Conceptuality is subjective; realization is objective."

Not knowing is uncomfortable for most, so the omnipresent uncertainty that reigns in the markets will often prompt traders to look at subjective modes of analyzes. These people will often base their decisions on triangle patterns, head and shoulders, wedges, measured moves, and what not. They will try to make sense of these formations, measure their angle, their width, etc. This is an art, and I would say, an inscrutable one.

Let's take that same coin and change the weight (of the weighted side) with every flip. At the end of a sample, your chances won't be 70% anymore – it might be anything, but it will be very difficult to get a reliable reading as you keep flipping, depending on how much weight you add or subtract.

When you trade subjectively, that is exactly what happens. Let's say, you assume that there is a definable edge to be found in chart formations. But since what constitutes a chart formation rests on a subjective interpretation of data (who can really describe accurately and objectively what a reliable head and should is, right?), if you keep trading, you never really get a value that is reliable and representative of an objective reading of past data.

So with this kind of trading, the rules of execution have to change because in absence of an objective way of looking at the past, the law of large numbers can't really apply. Since discretionary trading rests on abstract and highly subjective criteria (what looks like a head and shoulder formation for you, might look like something completely different for me), you have to be selective on the trades you place. Quality over quantity becomes of an utmost importance, hence you have to scrutinize, analyze, weigh, judge…

Now, I am not saying that this kind of trading doesn't work – I'm sure there are legions of traders out there who could prove me wrong. What I'm saying is that if trading for a living is something you want to pursue with the least amount of stress possible, you have to work on making your trading process simple and straight forward. You have to give up the fun and thrill of subjective trading in favor of a more consistent and objective approach.

I don't trade subjectively anymore. I don't spend my time trying to make sense of charts or trying to see patterns where there just aren't. I have failed many times precisely doing so, and with the kind of self-knowledge I have acquired throughout the years, I know that this way of trading is not for me.

Nothing about the project of systematic trading entails believing things based on incomplete or biased evidence. Your "edge" is either here, or it's not… you take it or you don't. Again, I've placed close to 4300 trades since 2007 (which is really nothing in the grand scheme of things), and from what I've observed, there is no reliable "edge" to be found in formations like triangles, head and shoulders, etc. It all evens out after enough number of trades. There might be a slight "edge" in those formations, but fighting for that by deciphering the charts and trying to read in between the lines, just for a modicum of pseudo-certainty, is almost not worthy of my time and energy.

I'd rather not know anything... I'm better off that way. I am more calm, serene, I have more time for myself and my loved ones. And above all, my well-being doesn't hang onto any market direction or trade outcome because I didn't put much time and effort trying to figure out where they're going or what an outcome will result in. My trading methodology and my expectations are in line with the way markets are: uncertain.

We tend to think that our decisions, opinions, assumptions, and beliefs are always forged by careful, rational, and objective consideration of ideas, facts, and parameters. But, the reality is otherwise. These are all based on our feelings and many cognitive biases which can have an uneasy relationship with facts – especially when money in on the line. The only way to counteract that is through a systematic process that is not based on faith or personal conviction but an objective process that can be described mathematically and statistically.

Trading for a living should be full-filling. What I don't understand is how people claim they want to trade for a living to break free from their 9-5 jobs. They claim they want the freedom to do other things in their life, but then when they start trading, they feel the need to stay in front of their screen all day. They feel they have to trade all the time, analyze, scrutinize... I say to hell with that! Why free yourself from your regular job only to become a prisoner in another way?

We hold on to this misconception that we have to "work hard" at finding our opportunities in the markets.

We are lead to believe that this equals positive trading results, so we spend our time doing that. We read books on Elliot waves, Gann, Fibonacci retracements, abstract patterns, measured moves, even though all of these books often contradict each other.

We stay glued to our computer screens watching the markets' every move for that additional little bit of certainty. We spend time on trading groups and forums, following others' calls so that we can avoid the pain of failure. No, my friend… this is not the right way to approach this!

"In its essence, trading is simple, but we insist on making it complicated."

Working hard gives us the impression that we are productive, that we are moving closer and faster towards our goals. But, in an endeavor like trading, working hard doesn't always land us expected results. Paradoxically, quite often, it makes us unproductive and inconsistent.

My advice to you: eliminate subjectivity from your trading approach. You don't need to know what is going to happen next, because if you have a very clear idea of what will happen, you tend to get very rigidly attached to it, then you shut out a whole range of other possibilities for that very trade.

When you get attached, you freeze your desire into a rigid framework which interferes with the whole process of having the numbers work in your favor.

Also, let go of trying to make trading for a living harder

than what it actually is! Instead, work on simplifying it. For instance, I have two accounts, a bigger one where I trend-follow stocks while holding them anywhere from a few days to a couple of months. Nothing magical about this, I just buy breakouts from horizontal bases, and I sell breakdowns. Then I use a combination of contingent orders to manage my trades. That is it!

In my smaller account, I typically day trade the spy, and occasionally other stocks, for quick cash. Same here, my strategy is objectively defined – only with the exception of taking profits. That way it's easier for me to refrain from judging, weighing, or even doubting for that matter. I just take my signals however they come.

This is not to say that I spend my days taking every signal I get. I spend maximum 2 hours a day doing that, then I'm done, regardless of profits or losses.

Easy!

And that's how it should be!

It's the only way that I've seen that reduces my emotional involvement and makes trading for a living a worthwhile endeavor. If it's not this way for you, then I suggest that you start working on a way to get there.

"You can't get positive results with a negative mind."

So, by now, we all know that a good trader trades his proven methodology – subjective or objective, but I hope I convinced you that an objective one is more consistent and less stressful. We also know that the good trader is an excellent risk manager.

However, it can't stop here, and my argument is that If it did, a lot more people would find durable success in the markets. At this point, trading would just be a game of applying a model to the letter. And we know empirically that a lot of people fail at doing such a simple and seemingly "easy" task. So there must be more to the story; there must be another *deeper* criteria that we're not considering.

Devising a methodology, one can argue, is the easy part. But, the mental aspect of trading is where most people struggle. It's one thing to have a methodology, but it's another thing to follow it during good and bad times. It's just not easy – especially if you're trading for a living! Just ask any genuine trader who does so and almost always you'll get the same answer: while a proven edge and an efficient risk management technique are building blocks, psychology – an appropriate state of mind when trading –, is what glues those blocks together!

There is a way of trading that is not contingent upon merely following the next discursive emotions, thoughts, and impulses that sap weeks, if not months, of work hard. There is a way of trading that can truly be fulfilling and pleasant as a matter of subjective experience. And this state of mind is available for anyone to experience, provided that we change our perspective on a few things. Let's delve right into that.

3. BEHIND THE CURTAINS

*"The mind is a fascinating instrument
that can make or break you."*

.

I am no neuroscientist, but I cultivate a deep interest in the "device" that stands between our two ears. I think, there is no other part of our body that is more important. The brain is all we have. It is that through which we interpret the world; it is the engineer behind our thoughts, feelings, personalities, hopes, fears, and aspirations. And the very fact that I am here writing this book, and you there reading it, depends on the integrity of this biological tissue.

Yet, the brain is utterly alien to us. Most of us live our lives without even a basic understanding of its inner workings. For instance, for the longest time, my mind was the cause of all of my troubles in and out of the markets, but it was never really clear for me that I wasn't actually using it properly!

To better understand what pulls the strings of our behavior so as to better transcend our limitations, I think it is useful to get a brief understanding of how this "device" works.

As much as we like to think that our body and mind are living separate existences, in reality, the mental is not separable from the physical. The brain is part of the body and our decision-making right to our very personalities can change in very specific ways when it is affected or altered by trauma – caused by painful past experiences, tumors, drugs, disease, etc..

"Body and mind are one reality!"

This might seem like a platitude, but it does clarify some aspects of our existence while deepening the mystery of others.

Neuroscientists have discovered that what takes place at the level of consciousness – the awareness of the "me" – is only a tiny bit of the operations the brain is processing. The large majority of the brain's activity resides in the vast unconscious and automated processes that run under the hood of conscious awareness.

This discovery has given rise to a better understanding of the multiple complex processes that make a person. A person is not a single entity of a single mind. We are packs of processes, all of which compete to steer the status quo of the ship that is our "selves." Physical, but also cognitive functions (all aspects of reasoning, thinking, evaluating, judging, remembering, and feeling) are dependent upon the how these processes interact with each other.

To further expand on this, let's take the neurophysiological processes of fear that run under conscious awareness. Fear is an instinct every animal possesses. It is intended to help us survive a dangerous situation by preparing us to either run or fight for our life (thus the term "fight or flight"). If it wasn't for fear, we wouldn't have survived for long. We would be eating those delicious purple berries even though they're poisonous. We would carelessly attempt to pat that sabre-tooth cat on the back...

Our brain records what is potentially dangerous to us in the form of a painful memory or an inherent inclination towards knowing that something might cause us harm or injury. Naturally it wants to keep us away from this possibly painful or life-threatening situation.

Neuroscience is revealing through brain scans the underlying stories of what is happening in our heads when we are in an apprehension of danger, and how our behavior is altered consequently.

For example, in the case of a painful memory, the mind never forgets important emotion-laden lessons. Short of injury or illness to the brain, history cannot be erased! Worse still, history has a way of popping into memory at the worst possible times.

It's while we have to let a winning trade run that we tend to recall that time when we lost all of our profits as we were doing so. We're most likely to recall our most traumatic loss just before taking a signal, as well as the profits we would have kept if we hadn't adhered to our stop-loss.

The brain is "referential" – it is programmed to notice similarities from one environment in another, perhaps completely different, environment. Example: if this dog bit me, then all dogs are dangerous and I shall avoid them. If this losing trade caused me emotional pain, then I shall avoid the memory and anything that evokes that memory.

That is the basis for our beliefs and the more the case can be made in favor of those similarities, the stronger the belief!

Humans can attach emotional content to thoughts, symbols, and memories in a unique way. We will show signs of distress when describing a past, painful experience, almost as if the thing itself is present, rather than the memory of it.

Sometimes the memory of a painful event can evoke more distress than the actual event itself did because the mind has this propensity to over-exaggerate things. For example: if it doesn't want you to take another loss, it will do everything it can to prevent you from doing so by commanding, sometimes, a plethora of discomforts – again for the sole purpose of survival!

Whenever a possibility of danger is sent to our brain via our 5 senses, in the space of a micro-millisecond, the brain makes a "chemical choice" about how to best protect us – from imminent death, physical injury, or the possibility of emotional pain.

"You become fearful the moment you identify with fear."

The mind has a simple response to what it perceives as danger: avoid, avoid, avoid! And how does it persuade us to avoid this? It tries to smack us with afflicting anxiety and discomforts.

In these precise moments, the brain releases cortisol. This toxic hormone and neurotransmitter floods the brain and shuts down its executive functions that help us manage the gap between expectations and reality. In other words, it induces cloudy thinking which prevents us from judging or reacting objectively in the presence of a difficult and stressful situation.

In the face of this disruption, the amygdala, our instinctive brain, takes over and we operate in fight or flight mode. When that happens, the element of objectivity and careful consideration slowly erodes and the brain will push us (through intense discomforts) to do what it, in fact, thinks is the best way to avoid pain, injury, or danger.

It will approach pain that comes from the inside (emotional) just as it approaches pain that comes from the outside (physical): it will try to control and avoid it at all cost! At this point, for us traders, our intentions go through the window and our plan right into the trash!

"Fear is the brain's way of saying that there is something important for you to overcome."

So why does this brain stuff matter? And what does it have to do with detachment? Again, how can you expect durable changes in your behavior if you can't make sense of why you do what you do? For me, it's a no-brainer (pun intended), and understanding this organ through which we experience the world is central. But, this stuff also matters because it illustrates the ways in which our primitive minds can be pitted against our higher, more rational minds.

The power of emotional and physical discomforts can overwhelm rationality more often than not. That is why when we are emotionally upset or stressed we can't think straight.

Without a clear understanding of the conditions that trigger a fear response within us, and an awareness of when it's happening, our minds are bound to keep playing the same track over and over again. There is nothing wrong with this – the brain is just doing its job. This survival mechanism is obviously there for a reason, but in trading, it can come at a high cost.

The mind, in the face of "danger", doesn't have the most accurate view of the world — we're often smacked for dangers that are illusory and not even present it the moment. And there is a reason why the mind has such a skewed view of things. It is an expert at remembering bad experiences, and it will always come up with one more example of why it is right.

When the mind is operating in this mode, it doesn't matter how hard you try to prove it wrong. It can always find one more piece of evidence in its favor, no matter how irrational the conclusion. For example, it can turn a Harvard education into evidence of failure. That is why the "fight your emotions" and "trade without emotions" sayings are by no means good pieces of advice. If you fight or argue with your mind, most of the time it will just end up making matters worse.

But, there is hope! You see, we are also wired to see beyond the mental afflicts to find a way out, to cope... if that were not the case, you wouldn't be reading this book!

"Everything you've ever wanted lies on the other side of fear."

There are beneficial (and worth knowing) questions to be asked about individual experience. Your experience of being who you are can be studied through self-inquiry. With such study, you can come to understand how you see the world, why you argue with yourself, how you fall prey to cognitive illusions and the unconscious data-streams of information that influence your opinions. For example, if you fear dogs, through self-inquiry you can begin to see what beliefs you are holding about dogs that make them so scary and also, in some cases, how you acquired them.

After this process of self-inquiry, it becomes easier to develop awareness. Awareness implies paying non-judgmental attention to your experiences. In essence, you're letting go of intellectualization and you're learning to see things as they are. Beneath all the logic, reasoning, and stories our minds create, fear and discomfort (as they are on a conscious level) are just images and maybe a little bit of language in the mind, followed by some mere physical sensations. That's all they are if you learn to see them as raw data, without actually feeling identical to them.

And the "knowing" that fear is just a bunch of processes happening in the brain below awareness can help us cultivate this sense of detachment from the feelings, thoughts, and sensations that are brought forth as a result of these processes.

It also helps to know that, thoughts, feelings, and sensations are transient – they come and go, and they always will because they are part of you. However, when you cling to them, you let them dictate your behavior.

Without cultivating a habit of detachment, those states will always appear to be who you are, in the moment. When you feel identical to everything that passes through your mind, you are, in essence, on autopilot, and you tend to mindlessly react in an unconscious attempt to make bodily discomforts and afflictive thoughts go away.

A reaction is automatic and draws upon unawareness and fixed beliefs based in fears. Overcoming this requires active awareness and self-inquiry – questioning in real-time whether this set of feelings, sensations and thoughts require being acted upon. Reactions result in a close set of options. As we've seen, it's the fight or flight response. Awareness, on the other hand, results in an open set of options.

Knowing when to let go of the stories your mind recalls becomes obvious once you begin developing conscious awareness. By the end of the book, you'll know how to cultivate such a habit.

Now that we've explored the brain (albeit, loosely), and introduced fear and its consequences, in the next chapters, I will discuss the effects it has on what we believe to be true about failure, money, and change. All of our problems as traders, from our high expectations to our sheer lack of confidence (or trust) in ourselves and our process, find their roots in those three themes. We'll also look at how we can begin to let go so as to better desensitize ourselves from our unfruitful behaviors in the market.

4. FAILURE

"In order to succeed, you first have to be willing to experience failure."

The highlight of what we do as traders revolve around courting uncertainty – it spins and turns, and we merely need to hold its hands and dance with it. But the traders who don't know the dance, or those who are instead leading a fight, are the ones who typically go home alone (and broke). That is exactly where I was a couple of years ago.

I started trading in 2007, but because of my inflexibility, 5 years into the endeavor and I still couldn't engineer consistent results. At one point, my financial situation became so dire that I had to make this work.

Unfortunately, things didn't conform to my hoping, wishing, or praying. Reality didn't fit the box-shaped vision I had for it. The pressure to perform, coupled with my fears of failure – which were instilled in me from an early age and strengthened through my painful life experiences in and out of the markets – made making money an impossible feat to achieve.

Later in 2011, I blew up and my whole world, which was already hanging on a thin string, came crashing down. I had failed to make it as a trader, and in my obsessive quest for financial freedom, I had alienated family and friends. I became more and more closed off, and I was in poor physical and mental health.

I had failed my life (so I thought).

Today, as I let those painful memories capture my experience of the present moment – while enjoying a nice cup of Yerba Mate in a beautiful cottage overlooking the gorgeous white mountains of British Columbia – I can only smile. Of course, nothing "bad" happened to me. Sure, I felt pain, but my life didn't end. I didn't lose my sanity, and I surely didn't give up on my dreams.

In fact, life is pretty good at the moment… I now make decent money in trading, and my books and occasional speaking gigs complement that income. But above all, I am healthier and definitely happier than ever.

So what happened?

A lot of things! To understand everything I went through, I'll let you read *Zero to Hero*. But in short, I changed my perspective on a lot of things and this started with a simple shift in how I viewed my failures.

"Fall seven times, stand up eight."

In dealing with some ingrained patterns of detrimental behavior – understanding their cause in order to better transcend them – we have to take an objective assessment of reality. And the reality of our negative perception (of failure) can be rather insidious as it finds its roots in the core of our society.

A lot of things are passed on to us through our genes, but the only fear that we acquire this way is that of falling. This is observable in young babies – they can't determine what is outside the norm and could be a cause for alarm but for the feeling that they are falling. So, many of the fears that we possess and express in the world, are passed on to us via our parents, culture, etc.. In other words, fear is learned, and this is especially glaring with our aversion to failure!

In the west, the classical way this fear is taught to us (and reinforced) is through our educational process, which came about not to really educate children but to develop good employees. The sole purpose was – and still is – to "create" highly skilled workers who are able to think and come up with new ideas, but they also have to do what they are told. This is achieved through the educational process where we are taught to never question the teacher, and to learn everything we are taught in a rather systematic manner.

We are fed with facts, tested on those facts, and those of us who make the least amount of mistakes are considered to be the smartest ones. The ones with the lowest scores are shamed and disparaged.

Hence, the educational system spends no time teaching us that failure is, actually, an essential part of the process of success. We aren't taught how to learn from our mistakes and how to rebound from failure – yet this is critical to real learning.

Unless you had exceptional teachers who were willing to break out of the mold, chances are that you weren't learning those crucial life lessons needed in order to navigate real life – let alone the markets.

Learning those lessons is part of life one might argue, and I agree with this proposition. But how can we learn if:

• Everyone around us is doing the same thing – trying to avoid painful experiences that come as a result of being wrong and failing?
• Everyone around us is striving for perfection, even when no such thing exist?
• Our parents couldn't even teach those lessons to us, because they, themselves, didn't learn them?

You see, it's a cause-and-effect relationship, and society as a whole marginalizes us if we don't live up to these same dysfunctional standards.

"Failure is only an opportunity to begin again – this time more intelligently."

This is less of a problem for the majority of the population who are fine working for someone else. But, for those of us who embark on a journey to becoming self-sufficient and self-directed traders, entrepreneurs, and innovators, we start our journey ill-prepared for the harsh reality that awaits us.

Instead of flowing with, and adapting to, uncertainty, we desperately try to create it even where it doesn't – and cannot – exist.

For us traders, we unknowingly crave the sense of certainty that analyzes and the numerous indicators on our charts appear to give us, and our egos hang onto every trade we place.

Up and down moves in the markets make our mood swing like a pendulum. And when we are proven wrong, lose, or miss, we freak out because according to what we have all learned to believe, failing means there is something wrong with us. Failure also means the end.

So, naturally, we insist and try harder to be right; to "succeed without failing" in order to feel whole, smart, responsible, virtuous, and safe... but it's a never ending cycle and a recipe for misery unless we learn to break out of it.

"Before the truth can set you free, you need to recognize which false belief is holding you hostage."

Our fear of failing comes from unconscious standards that we hold in our mind based on past painful memories.

We must have experienced shame, belittlement, humiliation, mockeries – often repeatedly – to have developed an aversion to it. And the mind, in a clumsy attempt to protect us, builds these rigid walls of expectations and standards. It automatically thinks that if it tries harder to be right, then it will spare us pain.

Again, as we see, it's a typical example of the fight or flight response in action. This response isn't only triggered when faced with the possibility of physical threat. It can be triggered when we are confronted with information that is contrary to our worldview or paradigm.

This "cognitive dissonance" arises as an extremely uncomfortable feeling at a discrepancy between what we already know or believe, and new information or interpretation. And the natural reaction is to protect what we already know to be true. Example: I am right in my assessment of market direction, therefore I will keep my trade on, even though the market has proven me otherwise. Even though the market is trending, I will exit my trade here for minimal profits because last time I lost money when I kept it on.

What is pulling the strings are those high standards or ideals that we hold for ourselves, and others, that we grew to believe and act upon.

"We only see what we are prepared to see."

Inflexibility breeds mediocrity in trading, relationships, and anywhere else, but acknowledging this fact allows us to play the game differently. We have to learn to let go of our need to be right in order to escape failure, and instead, embrace uncertainty and real growth. This is the only way to change our experiences, in and out of the markets, to something that is truly fulfilling as a matter of subjective experience. A mind open like the sky allows us to see that:

1. The control we think we have…. it's an illusion!
We live in a world of cause-and-effect and the reality of our lives is a direct result of causes (actual and prior) that we don't have any control over. It is determined by different factors, many of which are impossible to investigate. Do we have control over all the people, close and far; known and unknown, who affect our lives so intimately? Do we control the overwhelming power of nature? Do we have control over what markets do? This control we think we have on things is an illusion! And if it is so, then failures are bound to happen. But we can minimize their number of occurrences by keeping a growth mindset at all times and by staying open to the lessons they teach us.

2. As propounded in chapter 2, our cherished beliefs, opinions, values, and decisions are biased, however much we resist to defend them. We tend to think that they are forged by careful, rational, and objective consideration of ideas, facts, and parameters. We like to think they have the ring of intelligence and soundness to them. Of course, the reality is otherwise. Beliefs, opinions, values, and decisions are all based on our feelings and many cognitive biases which can have an uneasy relationship with facts. This is something to keep in mind whenever you feel like arguing with the markets. When all is said and done, price doesn't lie.

3. Interpretation happens within us. The environment that surrounds us (markets included) doesn't interpret the information it has to offer. Good, bad, right, wrong are subjective ideas and occur strictly in our minds. So, we are the ones putting context behind our experiences with our own sets of beliefs and values. But, it is possible to change how we live each and every experience. We just have to shift our perspective on what wrong really means for us. Does it mean guilt, shame, frustration, anger, despair, confusion, or intrigue, impartiality, incentive, opportunity to learn, inspiration, creativity? In any case, we create our own reality. If I could go back 10 years, just when I started trading, that is what I would tell to my younger self.

4. Success and failure are intertwined. Success is not an event, it is a process composed of valleys – failures, mistakes, losses. Take, for instance, the process of scientific investigation which human advancement rests upon. When a science experiment is conducted, many results will show up – positive and negative ones – all of which are data points. That is how scientists view failures – as just data points. When we adopt a similar approach, every winning or losing trades become data points. By this process of careful experimentation, as we keep trading, we discover more data around what works and what doesn't. That is the epitome of a scientific approach, which is conducive to better and stronger results in the long run.

5. We need "failure." The situations and experiences we like to resist with all our might are precisely the ones which should be embraced because everything that dismantles our limiting mental construct is beneficial. Failure is just an experience. We are here on earth to have experiences, aren't we? Our fears may come true, but even with a bad outcome, there may be good if we have the awareness to see it. Nothing is ever "wrong," therefore, we are safe at all times.

"Focus on what you can control, instead of what you can't."

When we cultivate a sense of stillness and ease in the midst of uncertainty, we allow things to happen the way they want to. And this letting go of trying, wishing, wanting, has the potential to engineer for us not only consistent trading results but also emotional well-being.

It shifts our perspective from one that is solely focused on not failing, and control, to one that is focused on learning, but above all enjoying ourselves in whatever we do and whatever happens. Most things aren't as serious as we make them anyways.

How does this translate in trading?

Let's say you have a trade on. You might desire a certain outcome for that trade. That is what you want. But what if you let go of this desire? What if you say, *"I don't know what will happen."* (By the way, you really don't). What if you say, *"Let's see what happens."* You place your trade; you put your contingent orders, and you let it work to fruition. Win or loss, it is what it is, but you fully trust your methodology – which structures your approach to the markets.

Now, this particular trade might turn out to be a loss but as you step back and allow things to happen, over time your results will take care of themselves, and your needs will also be met – minus the anxiety, frustration, and other limiting states of the mind.

As soon as your mind tells you that something always happens and that it is 100% right on the assessment of a particular situation, that means that you are in the grid of a false belief. Always is never true. At any moment, you have the chance to break out of this mode of thinking that is trapping you. You don't need to know, and you certainly don't need to be right to make consistent money in trading.

You have to trust me on this, things will surprise you if you just let them happen as they may! When we become the scientists of our own lives, we free our minds of the emotional stigma associated with mistakes, failures, and being wrong, and instead we let curiosity and opportunity enlighten our lives.

"Failure is just a matter of perception."

So ask yourself the question: are you genuinely trying to be successful or are you merely trying to avoid failure? Your answer to this question can shed light on the reality of the results you are engineering for yourself, in trading and otherwise.

As I conclude this chapter, I would like to signal an important point. Understanding (and knowing) what has been discussed so far merely signify intellectual realization. This is wonderful. However, there can be a big difference between that and practical experience. Only practical experience can emboss this realization in your mind as a core belief. In chapter 6, we'll talk about the importance of practicing what is uncomfortable (as hard as it is), and then in chapter 9, I'll show you a simple exercise that will serve as a constant reminder to let go, accept, embrace, and trust as you venture towards your trading goals.

5. MONEY

"The process by which one accumulates money is so simple, yet so hard to implement for most."

Since our goal is to make trading pleasant and fulfilling, and certainly as least stressful as possible, we have to find a way not to let winning trades go to our head and losing trades to our heart.

In the previous chapter, we have discussed how a shift in what we believe to be true about failure helps in that regard. Now, let's delve into the issue of money....

Consider this: picture a guy walking in equilibrium on a rope over the Grand Canyons. What do you think is happening in that person's mind?

• Do you think he is thinking about falling?

• Do you think he is thinking about reaching the end of the line ASAP?

• Do you think his attention is strictly on the process of keeping his balance and staying present with each and every move he takes?

I think the answer is clear: if the guy focuses on falling, in all likelihood, he is going to fall. If he focuses on reaching the end of the line as soon as possible, he also stands a greater chance of falling. However, if he focuses on the part that is in his control – staying present and focusing on the process of keeping his balance which he probably spent countless hours rehearsing – his action will become more faithful to his goals.

Similarly, in trading, we all want to make x amount of money in the markets, but this is out of our control. You don't get to decide what the markets ought to give you in each and every moment. Behaviors, by contrast, is something that you can control. They are the things you focus on in order to achieve your goals of earning x amount of money.

For instance, you set an intention out there that you want a certain amount of money or profit. This is your intention, you don't know if the markets are going to give you that, but you put it out there anyways. And every day you say to yourself, *"what can I do today that can set me closer to my intention?"* Then you forget the intention and strictly focus on your behaviors.

Of course, it's always useful to keep your expectations low, so low that you'll achieve it most of the time. But it's also important to acknowledge that you are never going to reliably get a specific amount that you decide upon – but your behaviors are going to help you get as close to it as possible.

"If your focus is on money, you will never improve your results. If your focus is on improvement, you will get the money."

When I stopped thinking about the money and started focusing on my behavior, everything changed for me – my stress and anxiety levels went down, and my whole experience of trading changed for the better. I suddenly realized that my wishing, hoping, wanting, was actually a grotesque misuse of my time and mental energy. Furthermore, I realized that this strategy doesn't work.

You control your entry, your exit, your risk level, your position size, etc., and your goal is to stick to your process in that regard. But the moment you shift your focus of attention from your process to the money (the need for or the lack thereof), you will begin to obsess over every single tick, and you will be inclined to check your positions every minute of the day. You will tend to take every market movement ad hominem, and you will mess with your trades in an unconscious attempt to make the discomforts go away.

I'm sure you have been through this scenario at some point: you go through a week where you trade well; you have had a lot of winners so this begets additional confidence and you keep doing all the right things. But then you enter a string of losses.

From this point, there is one of two things that happens:

This string of losses spoils everything for you, mentally! Your mind starts to doubt, judge, weigh, and you start deviating from your methodology. You start thinking about the money you lost and want back, and you drop your rules.

Or

You say to yourself, *"I'm proud of myself, I've been following my plan to the letter. Whatever the current results are, I will keep doing the right thing over what merely feels good."*

As you can see, one mode of thinking is "money-oriented", while the other is "process-oriented." Which one do you think will fare the best results in the end? Which one is less stressful and makes trading a more pleasant enterprise?

The answer is obvious. By choosing the "process-oriented" approach, you are building the results you want and the capacity to follow your plan in good or bad times. However, if you are operating with a "money-oriented" mode of thinking, you are approaching this whole endeavor the wrong way.

If you want to trade for a living and build a durable trading career, you can't allow winning trades to make you overly happy and enthusiastic, and losing trades to make you depress. It's a weakness to get caught up in both, and it's precisely what will cause you shoot yourself in the foot, all the while making trading for a living a miserable experience for you.

To put it plainly, when you trade, you have to empty your mind of any expectations you might be holding for yourself. That is the key to success in this field, and sadly, it is understood by few people.

"If your happiness rests upon what you expect from trading, you are doomed..."

Focusing on the process of trading is a must, but incidentally, there are instances where your beliefs about money will interfere with your ability to do so. And, it might be useful to investigate those beliefs, especially if your behavior is reliably affected in certain ways when money is on the line.

For instance, how money was experienced, perceived, and talked about by your family is likely to have played a significant role in forming your financial values and your beliefs about earning, saving, spending, and investing. It is also equally possible that your country's socio-economical state and your culture have impacted the way you feel about money.

I know this as a matter of personal experience. I grew up having an absolute adoration for money. That was the belief that was instilled in me by authoritative figures in my life and that is what I saw all around me. Naturally, I grew up thinking that my happiness was contingent upon having a lot of it. When I started trading, as you can imagine, those beliefs didn't serve me well. I was an emotional mess and I got smacked for it!

And the opposite is also true. People who despise money, and merely have a marriage of necessity with it, will often find themselves reliably committing trading mistakes of all sorts. Their aversion to money shouldn't be confused with detachment – those are two different things.

Letting go/ detachment is not synonymous to aversion because we cannot be free from that which we resist secretly.

So, we need a right balance in our appreciation of money. In a quest to disarm some deeply ingrained fear-based patterns of behavior born of some erroneous beliefs or values that we might hold, it helps to take an objective assessment of the reality of money and our relationship to it.

"Money is just something you need in case you do not die tomorrow."

Money is an idea! It is whatever we think it is. A lot of it does not automatically make us rich and happy, nor does a lack of it make us poor and sad.

In our current day and age, we are forced into an "either-or" proposition, whereby you are either for capitalism and its intended or unintended consequences, or you're against it. In my opinion, that's not the right way to look at this, and a deeper truth lies ahead of someone who truly seeks.

Surely the good life is contingent upon having a fat bank account. As I write this, I just arrived at the Four Seasons in Seattle. I am on a heavenly comfortable bed and on my left, through the window, is an amazing view over a bright and alluring heated pool. This is certainly a statement to the type of experiences money can buy.

But, there is a caveat which most of us ignore: if one's happiness is solely dependent upon external factors, then happiness will always seem elusive and ultimately unsatisfying.

Nothing lasts forever, that is why your well-being cannot solely rest on external factors, like money, bigger houses, trendier clothes, faster cars... even people. You have to learn to find a happiness that is not contingent upon anything or anyone else but yourself.

And, this brings us to the following question: would you trade if there was no potential for any monetary reward?

The vast majority of people wouldn't! In fact, they don't even enjoy their current day job. And they earn so little from it that they naturally start looking for alternative ways to bring in more money – to hopefully break free from their shackles while being able to afford the good life.

Then they learn about trading, and its possibilities in terms of financial rewards. This goads their eagerness and motivation to start a trading career.

This is all good. But the thing is that to survive in this business, you have to pour love into what you're doing – so much that money takes the second place in your mind.

This is very important to understand because trading is not like any other field where success is proportional to the amount of work you commit to it. Success in trading is proportional to how much you are willing to let go of your attachment to, and need for, money, success, but also certainty, comfort, etc..

I know it's a tough mental barrier to break – at least it was for me. But it's the reality of the situation. Nothing worthwhile can be achieved in the markets without undergoing this fundamental shift in approach.

This doesn't mean that you give up your intention to create that which you desire, rather you give up the attachment to the result or the money. The moment you do that, and you combine it with your intention and focus, the money will come, as a by-product.

Without detachment, we are prisoners of helplessness, hopelessness, despair, fear, anxiety, stress, trivial concerns, quiet desperation, all of which are the distinctive features of the unprofitable trader.

"If your happiness rests upon what you expect from trading, you are doomed."

So, I would suggest that you review what you believe to be true about money in a quest to better understand what is pulling the strings of your behavior. A pen, a piece of paper, and a little bit of silence can go a long way!

And whatever insights you gain about the nature of your beliefs, just remember this: being a trader is ultimately an act of thinking outside of the box. While the world feeds into this natural tendency we all have to focus on short-term emotional gratification at the expense of longer-term goals, we traders should embrace a different way of operating. In fact, if we want to achieve anything worthwhile, in or out of the markets, nothing is more important. With time, and repetition, we then expand our endurance and we become more competent to act in our best interest.

Pursue excellence, ignore success, and above all don't

take your winners and losers too seriously. If you do that, I promise you, your experience of trading will be much more enjoyable and you'll obtain far better results.

6. CHANGE

"There is no constant but change itself."

Let's continue our roundtable of the types of fears that prevent us from trading with a relaxed and impartial state of mind...

Right next, we have the fear of change that we need to address. As I keep reflecting on my journey as a trader, using the benefits of hindsight, I can clearly point out the things I didn't get right at the time. For instance, one of the fundamental lessons that I have learned (and come to accept) is that change is constant and no amount of wishing, wanting, and hoping will ever change that. In fact, there is nothing more important one needs to realize, as an individual first, and as a trader second.

Nothing is permanent except change, in the markets

and anywhere else, and this realization can initially be disconcerting, but as it settles in the mind, one can only notice its liberating qualities. When you notice that there is nothing to grab onto, your actions become more in line with reality and you liberate yourself from any resistance that might be pervasive and limiting.

Most people avoid change because they don't like the discomforts that are often associated with it. As the first signs of discomforts come careening into awareness, we run as fast as possible in the other direction.

However you look at it, the fear of change always boils down to one main concern: You! It is born of the thought that:

• You won't be OK if you venture outside of your comfort zone
• You are not good enough
• You risk losing something that is important to you

So, fear of change is a lack of trust in yourself and the present moment. You are, then, restricted to a small zone of comfort, and so, you can't fully take advantage of the opportunities present in the markets – in fact, you even pass on most of the best things in life.

It's a vicious cycle! Since you are fearful, you don't take your trades when you should; you don't exit where you should; and you end up doing things in between that mess up your opportunity.

And that mind of yours, it won't stop whining, judging, weighing, doubting, criticizing....

"Uncertainty is an uncomfortable

position. But certainty is an absurd one."

Many people can't trade well because they don't like to wait. They are control freaks and they like things to be moving on their terms. So waiting is painful for them – and I'm not talking about some Guantanamo bay type of torture, but a mere feeling that they are just not used to.

This was me a couple of years ago. I abhorred change and I certainly didn't like things that were uncomfortable. Of course, trading didn't work so well for me because it precisely required me to do the opposite of what I was comfortable doing.

Right after my monumental blowup, one day, I went on a meditation retreat. As I was "forced" to sit there, turn my attention within, and face my inner demons, I became more and more uncomfortable with what I saw and experienced.

The first few days into the retreat, I was in agony, so much that I came to the point where I was just about to pick up my stuff, leave, and never think of this atrocious experience again. In hindsight, I can only feel gratitude that I stayed because something major happened – and that thing completely changed the course of my life.

As I sat with my mind and its afflictive content, my awareness shifted from being entangled with the discomforts to merely witnessing them. I began observing thoughts, emotions, and sensations while not actually feeling identical to them.

For the first time, I began taking a deeper look into my inner landscape. The natural unintended consequence of this simple act is that I faced my fears. Also, everything about me – the good, the bad, and the ugly – was laid there, but I was just seeing but not gazing, touching but not grasping…

It's very difficult to explain the real depth of the experience I had, and the only appropriate word I can refer to is "oneness."

And there is nothing spooky or even magical about this word or phenomenon. It's a fundamental aspect of human experience which is at the core of every practice where there is a complete loss of self-interest or concern. We'll delve more into that a little bit later.

So, I learned to sit, watch discomforts, and when I did, incredibly, it wasn't too bad. My world didn't end, nor did my mind implode. I was just uncomfortable for a moment, but then life resumed.

Months after I came back from the retreat, I began trading again, and I watched the same processes of discomfort unrolling again into my awareness. Thoughts came in, along them emotions and bodily discomforts. Before, whenever this happened, I would almost always end up acting on my impulses. My mind would over-think and make up excuses for why I should exit a trade, keep it on, or not even place it for that matter. But then, again I gave in to the discomforts, I observed them impartially, in a completely nonjudgmental way – no good or bad labels, no association to past memories, and just being with them. Before I knew it, I had completely disarmed my discomforts.

I repeated this process for every other area where I experienced difficulties, and slowly, I discovered that being fine with discomfort was one of the single biggest discoveries of my newly changed life.

"The secret of change is to focus your attention, not on fighting the old, but on embracing the new."

Once and for all, neuroscience research has proven that the brain – once largely thought of as immutable and unchangeable after a certain age – is, in fact, a dynamic organ that changes constantly throughout the course of our lives, as we gain new knowledge and experiences.

This ability to change is referred to as neuroplasticity. Derived from the words "neuron" (nerve cells in the brain linked by synapses) and "plasticity" (the capacity to be shaped, moulded, or altered), neuroplasticity is the brain's potential to create neural pathways and to reorganize itself according to how it's being used – or not being used.

Areas of the brain that you use often are reinforced as they become bigger and stronger while parts that are used less frequently become smaller and less effective. For instance, every time you feel annoyed and frustrated with losses, the neural networks and the areas of the brain responsible for the experience are reinforced, and the structures that produce the experience of being "calm and cool headed" slowly fall by the wayside.

Neurons that fire together wire together, strengthening neural pathways that establish our habitual thoughts, behaviors, and reactive patterns, which then fortifies those same neural networks. This is why it can be difficult to feel better after long periods of stress, depression, etc..

The areas and structures of the brain that are active in

cognitive functions (all aspects of reasoning, thinking, evaluating, judging, remembering, and feeling) are active when we trade. Therefore, the mental processes that take place during this activity (including your thoughts, judgments, emotions, and attitudes) are reinforced. So, how you trade (whether you act impulsively, let your losers go out of hand, cut your winners short, take trades outside of your methodology) you are in essence training you mind in that kind of behavior.

But this goes further: whatever you think, perceive, and feel (whether unconscious or intentional) even when you're not trading, is training the brain to think, perceive, and feel in those same ways when you are trading.

It's insidious…. I know. But it also shows just how primordial psychology is — your attitudes, judgments, and inner dialogue. This might be slightly less of a concern for those of you who trade as a hobby for passive ROI. But if you trade for a living as I do, cultivating the right psychology at all times is simply more important than your market edge and your risk management technique.

"Change brings opportunity."

So, if you really want to make durable changes in your way of trading, amazingly, the simple act of being OK with change and discomforts is the solution. It also prevents you from falling in long-established neural patterns. Essentially, every time you prevail over your discomforts, these are tiny votes for the kind of person you want to be — one who reliably acts in his own best interests in the markets or the opposite of that.

But first, you need some additional insights into the

nature of your thoughts and emotions in order to ease that process of change. We'll delve into that in the next chapter.

What makes being a trader more amazing than working a "regular" job with a regular paycheck is that we take risks, we stumble, we don't know what is going to happen but we make the most of it. We not only venture into the unknown ... we dive in, headfirst.

When you think about it, taking risks, embracing change and uncertainty, and stepping outside of our comfort zone, this is the essence of living, and we, traders, are full into it!

Let go, accept, embrace, be present, change, take action. A cure for your trading woes.

7. THE NATURE OF THOUGHTS

"A lot of the resistances we experience are really only thoughts."

As you begin reading this sentence, I invite you to pay attention to everything that appears in your awareness — the sensation of your breath, the sight of this text, the feelings in your body, the sounds around you — for a mere sixty seconds without getting distracted by discursive thought.

It surely sounds simple. The truth, however, is that you will find the task nearly impossible. Even if you were promised a million bucks, you wouldn't be able to avoid thinking but for a handful of seconds, before your awareness would be submerged again by the flow of thought.

We spend our lives lost in thought. This is the natural tendency of the mind – it ruminates, jumps from thought to thought incessantly, and every passing thought appears to be who we are.

I am by no means denying the importance of thinking. Thoughts are part and parcel of our human condition. Our ability to think is at the very core of our evolution as a species. Our thoughts gave birth to arts, literature, science, philosophy, and so on. So clearly, the problem is not thoughts themselves but, I argue, the habitual state of thinking without being fully aware that we are thinking.

Our failure to recognize thoughts as transient appearances in awareness is a primary source of human suffering, and certainly it is the reason why most of us can't reliably act in our best interest in trading.

Thoughts are predominant aspects of human experience. Everything we've discussed so far, from fears and expectations to fixed beliefs and goal-oriented focus, all of these attributes manifest themselves through thought, and this drives emotions, behavior, and the subsequent sets of thought. It's a never ending loop and an engine where the off-switch is practically non-existent.

"You must first realize the limitations of your own mind before you can transcend them!"

What caused me to look deeper into the nature of my thoughts is my own inability to manufacture consistency in my trading results, despite having a promising trading methodology.

I couldn't get myself to do what I knew I should do for the sake of my long-term results because of the constant afflicting thoughts and emotions that were driving my behavior. In that sense, I was a prisoner of my own mind.

I spent my time:

• Creating excuses for why I couldn't follow my methodology, and I almost always I placed the blame on something or someone other than myself. Actually, this was my forte!

• Wishing I had what others have, resenting them for their successes, and repudiating the reality of my life.

• Finding problems everywhere instead of opportunities.

• Doing everything I could to avoid the pain of being wrong.

• Dreading things that were out of my control for fear of having to go through failure.

• Giving priority to short-term emotional gratification instead of privileging my longer-term goals.

And so on

These pervasive habits defined who I was because I was identifying with the stories my minds created. This generated stress and anxiety; exacerbated my fears, and made me miserable in and out of the markets. And I didn't know there was an alternative to that. In essence, I was stuck in a cage that is wide open.

I think it's interesting and somewhat encouraging to know that our own experiences of our minds are no different than the minds of others. We're all plagued with the same thought processes – the patterns and habitual tendencies are inherently the same.

One day, I unintentionally realized the insubstantiality of my limiting thoughts. I began seeing that I was, in essence, held hostage by my own thinking. The sheer automaticity of my thoughts – just not being able to stop the inner conversation – became intriguing to me, so much that I began spending more and more time in isolation, whether through special retreats or solo wilderness expedition trips, in a quest to discover more about the happenings in my mind.

Eventually, through a simple practice called Vipassana, which entails sitting and paying strategically attention to the breath, I began seeing substantial changes in the way I perceived things. In these moments of fresh look, the empty nature of thought became more and more apparent to me. This is not to say that I was able to control thought – and that is not the point. What started happening is that I began accepting my thoughts, seeing them as they arise, and witnessing their passing.

This ability to see thoughts as nonsolid, transient appearances, and notice them as they arise, as opposed to being captured by them, has been the all-important difference since it has helped me engineer consistent trading results year after year. And these changes did not only pertain to the markets, they also affected my personal life in major ways.

"The voice and the images inside your

head are not who you are. You are the one who witness them."

What is a thought? No one really knows, but the point of this question is not to come up with an answer. It is to direct the mind to look into the very nature of thought – not the content, what it's saying, but what the thought is as a phenomenon.

This simple introspection exercise is something very few people do in their lives. Mostly we are just lost in the stories of our thoughts and we take the content to be all too important. That is why we make trading so hard and challenging when it shouldn't be the case. You don't lose sleep over a game of Monopoly, do you? (I hope you don't). Yet, with trading, we are so involved in the stories our mind creates around it, that it becomes practically impossible to perform from a detached and impartial standpoint.

What is startling is just how much power unnoticed thoughts have over us. For instance, we might be watching an unfolding move in the markets, and in a moment, the mind decides to hop on a train of association to thoughts and emotions. We don't know we're on this train and we only realize it in hindsight – after a costly trading mistake born of this association.

Thoughts are like little bullies in the mind, and they dictate behavior. *"Go here... go there", "Do this, do that", "You're not good enough.. you'll never be good enough", "Are you stupid? Don't enter this trade, you'll wind up losing again"...* It's just an endless barrage of opinions, judgments, comments, and they run our trading and our lives when they are left unchecked. But as soon as we pay attention to their nature, we see that they are a little more than nothing. They are pretty much insubstantial, empty, and illusory. One moment they are here, and the next they're gone.

Thoughts are like clouds, they have no tangible reality or intrinsic existence at all. There is, therefore, no logical reason why thoughts should have so much power over us. There shouldn't be any reason why you are enslaved by them.

When we recognize the emptiness of thoughts, the mind no longer has the power to deceive us. But as long as we take its content all too seriously, and as long as we think of our deluded thoughts as real, they will continue to torment us mercilessly, and trading under those conditions can only be a losing game.

There is tremendous space and openness when we are not enslaved by our inner conditions. So cultivating an awareness of our thoughts, I think, is the most important exercise a trader can do as he ventures in his journey to profitability.

Being aware of the quickly passing thoughts; being aware of the more pervasive ones; noticing where we pick those thoughts up; discerning the difference between skillful and unskillful thoughts, and seeing into thought's empty nature, all these initiatives can lead us directly into a profound understanding of how to work with our emotions.

"Holding onto anger is like drinking poison and hoping the other person to die."

As we all know, emotions are complex experiences. An emotion involves thoughts, sensations, physical afflicts, colorations of the mind, and how well we recognize emotions, as they arise in the present, depends on our level of awareness. For most people, awareness – of thoughts and emotions – is a completely unfamiliar aspect of experience. These people live their lives doing all kinds of things, not even recognizing that there is an underlying emotion that might be driving it all. They can't think of themselves as being separate from their emotions, or their thoughts for that matter... and it's very sad.

It is sad because these people live their lives not knowing that there is an alternative to being at the mercy of discursive feelings and emotions – and this alternative promises better psychological satisfaction. As long as we're not open to feeling and seeing our emotions, we live very defensively – we cannot guide our actions with objective reasoning, thus tempering the primitive area of the brain that is always trying to protect us from imminent dangers, even when there are none.

Let's take a simple example. James is a forex trader who has a losing trade on his hands. Instead of inquiring about the nature of that loss (is it born of a trading mistake; is it a result of the normal fluctuations in his methodology), he snaps at the markets in anger and breaks his keyboard. This is the third keyboard he breaks this month.

There are a few things to note here:

• Clearly, James is angry and frustrated, but responding in anger will not likely help the situation. In many cases, it will only worsen it! James is probably having a bad day and he certainly sees this loss as the cause of this.

• Even if he has a legitimate point to make about how this loss could have been avoided, he could take a step back and view the issue constructively and objectively – and certainly not blame the markets (or even himself for that matter). Whatever caused the loss, the only constructive way to look at it is through the lens of understanding, patience, impartiality, flexibility, and certainly not anger, frustration, and disappointment.

• In all likelihood, James will want to respond to his losses with another *revenge* trade – just to feel right again, and whole. But responding this way, especially through the lens of anger, won't help. If he can let go of the anger or frustration response (which naturally comes up), he can respond calmly and constructively. But, how can he reliably do that when he doesn't even know what awareness means?

• It's not the markets' responsibility to accommodate him. As much as he would want to, James can't force anything upon the markets. However, he can change his own response, which is his responsibility if he ever wants to change his experience of trading to something that is easeful and smooth.

Then there are other people who may recognize when emotions are present and arising, but they are deep into habituated patterns of being drowned in them.

Let's see an example of that:

Eric trades U.S stocks. He has a trade on with open profits and he wants to let it run for maximum profits. He pertinently knows that is what he should do based on the evidence at the moment. However, he is conflicted about it as he recalls his previous painful loss.

Eric knows that he is experiencing aversion, but part of him thinks it's legitimate since he doesn't want to get hurt and disappointed again by a losing trade. He also knows on an intellectual level that he should let this trade run, however, he is completely unable to detach himself from all the processes that lead to the construct of aversion. He may gain awareness of this emotion (and the discomforts associated with it) in the midst of it, however his level of awareness is not polished enough to make him snap out of it.

So even though he witnesses the opportunity in the markets to let his trade run (which he initially does), he ends up taking the trade off and at the wrong moment – on a retracement.

So as we see, Eric is taking is thoughts and emotions and feelings all too seriously, and he is untrusting of his trading process. And this patterns of behavior, repeatedly carry him on a train of association with thoughts and emotions.

If we are not mindful right at the moment we put a trade on, during that trade, and finally, after the trade has been exited, thoughts appear, easily trigger emotional responses and the behavior that usually follows. For both James and Eric's respective cases, what is so perplexing is how quickly this phenomenon of being captured happens – how thoughts, in many cases can condition different emotions without us even being aware of it. And all of this often happens even though the markets, in this present moment, bears no relationship to what happened in the past, except as a thought in the mind.

Awareness is something that is practiced and refined until you're able to see thoughts arise and you see them for what they are. This also has the benefit of revealing the impersonal nature of emotions. Physical discomforts, colorations of the mind, those are just automatic and contingent processes in the brain and the body that are linked together. However strong the discomforts, we need to look into these processes with objectivity so that we can be mindful of our impulses, rather than unknowingly get caught in them.

"We can't stop thinking... so might as well think positive."

Whatever we think of and ponder over, that will be the inclination of the mind. Frequent repetition of thought patterns and emotional states actually strengthen the neuro-pathways in the brain, which makes it easier for the same kind of thoughts and emotions to arise again and again, and each time, a little bit stronger and more anchored in your character than ever before.

So ask yourself this question: what pathways do you want to strengthen? If you are not paying attention to what you are cultivating as thoughts and emotions, very often (and unknowingly), you are strengthening the patterns that leads to more suffering for yourselves and more mediocrity in your trading results.

It takes a special kind of awareness to change your experience of trading (even more so of living) to something that is truly full-filling. This special kind of awareness allows you to see skillful and unskillful thoughts and emotions, discern which one is better for you so that you can abandon one and cultivate the other. In the next chapter, I will discuss about it – and what it entails – and in chapter 9 I will show you one exercise that you can do every day, that will allow you to develop an ability of discernment and detachment, so that you can experience a way of trading that is not contingent upon thoughts or emotions.

8. THE BASIS FOR AWARENESS

"Awareness is like the sun. When it shines on things, they are transformed."

Ok, so at this juncture, you now understand how your beliefs become your predominant thoughts. You also understand how your thoughts birth your emotions, your emotions your actions, your actions your habits, and your habits your destiny. And hopefully, you have a better appreciation for just how important detachment/ letting go/ acceptance is to the project of not only trading but life itself.

But how can you develop such a habit?

Furthermore, how do you train your mind to gain awareness of your thoughts and emotions as they are arising?

To these questions, there is one simple answer: mindfulness!

In its essence, the word mindfulness means 'to remember the present moment,' and the practice, in a nutshell, is one of paying non-judgmental attention to that specific moment. More often than not, the mind stays stuck in the past, so much that most of us do not know how to live in the present. We walk forward with our back facing the front, and to make matters worse, we are also slightly ahead of ourselves as we lean forward in anticipation of the future. Thoughts sneak up on us, and before we know it we're carried away by this stream of mental proliferation. Mindfulness, if developed into a solid practice, is a radical way to help us liberate ourselves from this incessant tug and pull from one thought to the other.

How does this help with trading? As we've seen in the previous chapter, it is helpful to begin noticing thoughts that arise when we trade, and for those thoughts, the different emotions that usually follow. For instance, a thought of how the markets have harmed you in the past might give you an immediate arousal of anger, aversion, hurt, or whatever it might be. A thought where the markets have rewarded you for following your methodology might give you an elongated feeling of confidence and trust. Those patterns happen again and again in the mind, and mindfulness helps us take awareness of when they are happening so as to cultivate the state which promises less psychological resistance, and equanimity.

During the last 4 years, my own practice of mindfulness has evolved so much – I've come to develop a profound understanding of the practice, its attributes, benefits, but also the often understated effects of its application. In exploring different strategies of working with discursive thoughts and pervasive emotions, I have expanded my understanding of what really works and what doesn't. I have tried almost everything, from affirmations to visualizations, and none of these got me the kind of results I got from a consistent mindfulness practice. And the reason is simple: mindfulness digs below our issues – which have roots in the construct of the "self."

"The ego is a construct of the mind, born of thoughts."

Whether we're talking about fears, beliefs, values... everything arises in consciousness as thoughts and emotions that we identify with. For the untrained mind, it is difficult to imagine that such thoughts and emotions are anything but you. However, when one practices meditation long enough and turns his attention inwards, this illusion breaks down and what is left is a true insight into the selfless nature of consciousness.

Our sense of "self" (commonly called the ego) is a construct born of our thoughts of past (the self as remembered in the past) and our thoughts of future (the self that is projected or anticipated as being in the future). Along with those thoughts are a plethora of emotions and feelings. When you pay attention, you begin to realize that the content of your mind and the bodily afflicts are not you. In other words, thoughts, emotions, sensations, feelings, all these things are experienced in the space of consciousness, and you – the real you – are merely an observer amidst all those states and changes.

The Self is not some spiritual abstract concept, it simply refers to the part of you that is identified with the mind-body. It's the part of you that is identified with thought and the main purpose of this evolutionary trait is preservation – both self and genetic preservation.

A couple million years ago, humans were prey to saber-toothed cats, cave bears, and an onslaught of potential hazards. Our ability to think and use past experiences to anticipate the future has allowed us to outlast those dangers, but evolutionary psychologists will tell you that we are still on a constant lookout for the things that want to eat us next. It is not something we consciously think of but it drives our behavior!

The trouble is that, in our current day and age, the markets are not a bunch of razor-toothed animals. If anything, they are here to offer us an opportunity. But it's fair to say that, being plagued by stress is a sure way to turn that opportunity into risk, and sabotage your own success.

Hence, there's a specific function for mindfulness and it has relevance for how we can work with our range of thoughts and emotions so that we can begin to see them for what they are: transient, ever-changing, impermanent... This gained insight into the nature of things (referred to as Vipassana) is a characteristic of mindfulness.

"The highest form of human intelligence is the ability to observe yourself without judging yourself. In essence, this is mindfulness."

Mindfulness is the ability to observe yourself in a non-judgmental way, therefore, effectively it is the guardian of the mind. There is nothing spooky or new age about that. In fact, everything I have discussed so far is backed by neuroscience (see notes and references). When you practice taking this observer stance, you are able to detach yourselves from unskillful thought patterns, and you are led to acknowledge that you are here, in the present, as much as your thoughts want to convince you otherwise. And the present and its circumstances are rarely as bad as our thoughts paint them to be. The present is not changed or colored by our painful memories. The present is, and will always be, the present, with its unique opportunities.

For instance, think of something.... Let say your biggest and most painful trading loss. See if you can embrace it. No matter how discursive and emotionally driven your thoughts are, just notice how you are simply noticing them. See how you are never actually taking the form of those thoughts, or emotions, or sensations. They just appear in your awareness. The 'you' beneath those conditions is not caught in any turmoil. That is what mindfulness does! Insofar as you apply it in your daily life, in each and every moment, in or out of the markets, it provides you with a new degree of freedom so that you can transcend your limiting behavior born of your fears, beliefs, and patterns of pervasive thoughts.

When you practice being present – not half present but fully present – you bring in all of you, even for a few seconds at a time, but certainly as much as you can. And when you do this in trading, it taps you into what you need most at the moment, what you need to know, and what you need to do, rather than mindlessly act on a feeling.

"The mind is everything. How you use it determines your reality."

What I talk about is not ground-breaking in any way – it has been said in many different ways, by many different people already. And its essence is that it's really about "relationality," or the way of being in relationship to experience – inner experience and outer experience.

Some people are really good at that. They are just so good at just observing the content of their mind that they are able to accomplish incredible feats. Take Wim Hof for instance, holder of 20 Guinness World Records for withstanding extreme temperatures. He has climbed Everest and Kilimanjaro in only shorts and shoes, stayed comfortably in ice baths for hours, and ran a full marathon in the highest desert (122 Fahrenheit) with no water and food. The man is a perfect archetype of someone who has mastered his mind to such an extent that fear, stress, discomforts, feelings, thoughts, emotions, are just information for him. They bear no weight in his judgment other than knowing that they are passing!

And this kind of mastery of the mind is not just reserved for the "talented." Talent helps but it is not the determining factor. What is, is a will to change, perseverance, commitment... It's something that you have to build and cultivate every day. There is no free lunch, but anyone can achieve that and, I argue, nothing is more important in trading. It overrides system and risk management, and it is the core of every durable success in trading.

"If you think you don't need to meditate, then you probably need it twice as much."

Cultivating a mindfulness practice is not easy, but ask yourself: *"What's the alternative?"* If you want to be present in your life and engineer better results for yourself, in trading and anywhere else, you have to take the plunge. Right now and in every moment, we all have this capacity to become better versions of ourselves, but all too often we get entangled in the stories in our minds.

Our resistance to committing to a regular practice is itself a by-product of our thoughts which we identifying with. I suppose that is the kind of dialogue that is happening in your mind at this moment: *"Oh yeah, I heard about the importance of mindfulness, I'll be more present in the future."* If it is, just know that you won't make it to the end of the hall before you revert to your old ways. But if you develop a daily practice, right now, without waiting, you will prevail. The process of change is not about later, it's about starting now!

In the next chapter, I'll talk about my daily meditation practice. You are free to implement it and make it your own, but feel free to inquire about others. There are lots and lots of ways to meditate, and in my humble opinion, the form doesn't really matter. What matters is the insights born of the technique, which all of them lead to. So again, our concern is not to find a perfect form of meditation — it's to form a daily habit!

Let's get right to it.

9. CULTIVATING YOUR MENTAL EDGE

"The secret to developing a strong mindfulness practice is showing up."

We get tons of training in thinking and problem solving, but we never get any training in awareness. Yet, awareness is more often than not the prelude to any kind of solution to our problems. Fear, anger, frustration, despair, confusion, crises, and even wars, all these things are spawned by the ego, which itself is a by-product of our thoughts.

So thinking, while being absolutely beautiful, can become an issue, and a pretty complicated one if you ask me because we simply can't escape it. Even Mother Teresa, widely considered as the most selfless human being that ever lived, had an ego. If she was able to think, she most definitely had one!

Thoughts and emotions are our evolutionary trait, and they're a by-product of our inclination for self and genetic preservation. They are there to steer us away from potential dangers, and they're very persuasive at that. Thoughts weight us down and they won't even let us go to sleep sometimes. This creates huge amounts of stress, anticipatory anxiety and the emotions that come with them. So what if we created a training in awareness? That is what mindfulness is!

Mindfulness is the awareness that arises from paying attention on purpose, in the present moment and non-judgmentally. Now there are many other definitions of mindfulness, and Buddhist scholars even have lots of different arguments about its importance and where it sits in the entire Buddhist canons.

But that's only irrelevant because we're not interested in the religious aspect of it. Mindfulness, as it is, is just brain exercise. Nothing more. You can add the religiosity to it if you want, and it's entirely up to you, but this book is about trading, so we're only interested in the practical aspect of this contemplative tradition.

"The point of mindfulness is to discover that it is something you already have. You don't acquire it, you just discover it."

The human brain is unarguably the most profoundly complex organ in the body, and 90% of its activity occurs beneath conscious awareness. This means that, even though we think that we have some control of how we think, feel, and behave, neuroscience suggests that it isn't so simple.

The concept of neuroplasticity is a new and exciting area of science. It highlights that our brain is constantly being reshaped throughout our lives by both our experiences and our thoughts. As stated earlier, we now know that it is the focus of our awareness that determines which brain networks is strengthened and which are weakened, or even lost. Therefore, when we get caught up in cycles of fear, worry, irritability, these are the networks in the brain that become stronger. So the more we fear or worry, the better we become at it.

However, on the other side of this, if we practice being calm, clear, and focused, we can strengthen these networks too. As humans, our brains differ from other animals. This is mostly due to the front area of the brain called the frontal lobe – often called the new brain as it was the last to develop in our evolution. When well developed, these parts of our brain help us to manage our strong emotions and respond with flexibility even when we feel overwhelmed. It also helps us tune into the feelings of empathy and insight.

When we worry, fear, or stuck, or overly focused on the money, our brain functions are more strongly dominated by the old brain, and specifically the amygdala. Again, the amygdala manages the powerful flight and flight response which switches on when we feel stress, anxious, and it releases hormones and chemicals – cortisol and adrenaline. That is why stress has such a big impact on us.

Hence with mindfulness, we are developing a way to help us manage this process more effectively by building our skills of attention, concentration, and the capacity to direct our awareness in a certain way. So, we are less likely to be swept up by strong emotions and the power of the amygdala. It also means that we can bring choice to our emotions and our thoughts, and in doing so, we are playing an active role in changing how our brain develops, in much the same way we can change the shape of our body by doing certain exercises at the gym.

When we practice meditation regularly we become aware of thinking and emotion. As our mind becomes more settled, our nervous system is able to take in more accurate information for flexibility, creativity, and clear thinking which enables us to manage challenging situations more skillfully. When we build skills of mindfulness, we still feel negative emotions and feelings like frustration, sadness, disappointment, fear, irritability... but the research shows that we recover much more quickly. We also know that regular meditation practice reduces the size of the amygdala, levels of stress hormones, and strengthens connections to frontal lobes. This all means that we're more likely to live with less stress and more happiness.

"When we learn to let things be, they gradually lose their power to disturb us."

Let's see how to develop a mindfulness practice:

First of all, commit. Many say that they don't have enough time to practice meditation. But it's not about time, it's about diligence to practice and the way you shift your priorities. If trading for a living is truly important to you, you will find a way to make it happen.

Check your expectations. Just like in trading, when we practice mindfulness with the expectation of obtaining something from it, what we expect has fewer chances of happening. So, keep this in mind: it's a process, not a goal.

Find a quiet spot. It really doesn't matter where you sit as long as you can sit without being bothered.

Pick a time and trigger. Not an exact time but a general one. For instance, meditate in the morning when you wake up, or at night. The trigger should be something you already do regularly, like brushing your teeth, or arriving home from work. For instance, every day I get up, meditate, shower, eat breakfast, and then I turn on my computers on. Always in the exact same order. That's the triggers I have developed. When I wake up, if I start my day without meditating, I won't feel good. I will tend to be a little bit less present in the following activities that I do and my day will seem a little bit more stressful.

Sit in front of a wall (optional). The wall is a metaphor for the difficulties we all face in life and sitting facing that wall allows us to face our difficulties. If we can cultivate equanimity while we are facing the wall, then nothing prevents us from doing the same thing when we are faced with difficulties in life.

Sit comfortably. How you position your body has a lot to do with what happens with your mind and your breath. You are free to choose whichever position you are more comfortable with. The most effective positioning for my body for the practice of meditation is the stable, symmetrical position of the seated Buddha. I use a zafu – a small pillow – to raise my behind just a little so that the knees can touch the ground. With my bottom on the pillow and two knees touching the ground, I form a tripod base that is natural, grounded and stable.

Put on a timer. If you are just starting out, 2 minutes

will do. You can increase your time when you have been used to sitting for a while. My practice has evolved to a point where I now sit for 20 minutes in the morning and 30 minutes at night. Commit to just 2 minutes a day for at least 2 months.

Choose the positioning of your hands. In my practice, I fold them in a position called the cosmic mudra. The right hand is held palm up holding the left hand which is also held palm up so that the knuckles of both hands overlap. The thumbs are lightly touching, thus, the hands form an oval, which can rest two fingers below the belly button. The cosmic mudra is there to help turn your attention inward. But you're free to just place your hands on your legs.

Close your eyes. Gradually become aware of the sensations of sitting. How does it feel? How do you feel in your body? How does it feel on your back? How about your legs? Don't analyze or judgment, just witness. Perhaps take a few deep breaths. Allow gravity to settle you into your seat. Gradually become aware of the process of breathing. Notice where you feel the breath – is it at the tip of the nose or is it at the rising and falling of the belly? Or is it both? Feel the sensations, from the beginning of the inhalation to the pauses, and then to the exhalation. Just simple cover your breath with your awareness. Let it come and go naturally. The moment you see that you are lost in thoughts, simply observe those thoughts, whether they are images; things you are saying to yourself; past, future, sensations, whatever it is, just observe! Notice how they disappear, and then come back to the sensations of breathing. What are the sensations you feel in your body? Again, don't spare in judgment, simply observe. You will get lost in thoughts again and again. It's totally fine. Notice! Observe. See how the quality of your breath is congruent with your state of mind. Mind and breath are one reality: when your mind is agitated, your breath is agitated; when you are nervous, you breathe quickly and shallowly; when your mind is at rest the breath is deep, easy and effortless.

In essence, what you are doing is that, with every thought that comes into your awareness, you are learning to let go, which starts with letting be, and you are strengthening your ability to do so.

With enough practice, you will begin to notice thoughts' transient nature, even more so their insubstantiality. You will be better equipped to transpose this habit of mindful awareness into other areas of your life – when you're trading, in traffic, and anywhere else.

At this point, you would have developed an ability to detach yourself from unfruitful patterns of behavior, but also things in general that are unproductive and not conducive to your well-being.

If that is not freedom, then I don't know what is!

10. LETTING GO OF TRADING

"One of the hardest decisions you'll ever face in life is choosing whether to walk away or try harder."

Every day, millions of people approach the markets the same way: they want to make a living as self-directed traders. This is very praiseworthy, but it doesn't happen with a snap of fingers. It's a process composed of a lot of valleys at the beginning, and many people are ill-prepared for this reality.

So, I thought I shouldn't end this book without raising the possibility of letting go of trading altogether. It's a very tricky situation to be in because all too often we tend to quit at the wrong time just when success is about to point its head. Hence, this is definitely something to consider before calling it quits, but I think it is also important to know when to quit – and there are certain signs that show that quitting is better for you in the long run...

• If you are consistently more frustrated than otherwise, you have to consider doing something about it, and this can encompass quitting. Trading cannot be consistently more frustrating than rewarding, and if it is, then something is wrong. At this point, it's best to stop and reassess.

• If you can't envision a possible solution for your constant failures in the markets, it may be time to quit. If you've been working on getting better at trading but you still have no confidence things will change, quitting might be the wisest thing to do, especially if you haven't invested (or lost) much yet.

• If trading keeps you from spending time with your family or seriously damages your well-being, it's a huge red flag. The way I see it is that trading should be an activity that provides you with the freedom to do other more fulfilling things in your life, like spending time with your partner, kids, and doing things that feed your mind and soul. If trading makes you prisoner of your computer screen, then something isn't right.

• Your current financial situation, as a result of your trading activities, is taking a toll on your mental and/or physical health. It is not normal to wake up at night because a losing position is on your mind. It is not normal to stay glued to your screen all day. And it is surely not normal if trading traps you into a negative state of mind.

"Don't quit because something went

*wrong. Quit because you tried your
hardest and nothing made it better."*

Now, let me nuance this by recounting my personal story...

In 2011, my lack of success almost drove me out of trading for good, but instead I decided to take a break from the markets for an undetermined period of time. As it turns out, this was the most important step I took as a trader.

Taking a break allowed me to:

• Rest
• Gain perspective
• Gain objectivity
• Work on my game
• Save up some trading money
• Fine-tune my plan, rules, and back test them
• Reformulate my intentions
• Reflect on my failures and analyze their cause

Late in 2012, I was back in the markets and more ready than ever to make it work this time. With an awareness of my behavior and the causes of my prior failures, came an element of choice (which I didn't have before) but also confidence   and   determination.

2013 was my first profitable year in the markets. It is also the year where I came in 2nd in a live trading competition. I've been consistently profitable ever since.

So again, as stated earlier in the book, the key question to ask yourself is this: *"Do I love trading?"*

Think about it: so many people are locked in jobs they hate because they haven't found that one true passion. They are good at certain things, so that is what they do here, there, but they aren't sure what that one thing they want to do forever could be.

My point is that, once you find that one true passion – that one big thing – you will pour love in it and you will find ways to maximize your experience of it. You will find a way to make it work for you regardless of how hard things might seem at times! While you may take pauses to reassess, quitting for good won't be something that is even remotely possible.

"Success is where preparation and opportunity meet."

A pause can offer you the opportunity to start afresh. And, in spirit of what has been discussed till now, as you work towards your dreams, remember this:

Learn to let go of the past

Many times we are held back by the slime of our previous failures and painful experiences in the markets. And this brings forth various shades of emotions, negative thought patterns, and mental barriers that affect behavior. Although we can make an intention to start clean, we can rarely sustain change if we cling onto what holds us back.

What we have to tell ourselves is that all this is old baggage now! They don't serve us, so why keep them? A fresh start demands a clean slate. Let everything from the past go.

Don't let yourself get caught up in old and unproductive habit patterns again. If you want different results this time, you have to start doing things differently! Let go of attachments to what you've been doing so far. Let go of failures, mistakes, painful trading experiences. .. even good ones. A clean slate is a clean slate.

Let go of fears you've built up. Let go of reluctance. Let go of your ideas about what trading has to be like, or what the markets have to look like. Let go of long-held beliefs and habits that don't serve you well.

Cultivate happiness, even when you lose

Don't look at happiness as something that will come when you have a winning trade, or when you've attained a certain accomplishment or certain amount of wealth or material possessions. Don't look at well-being as a destination, something that you'll get later. I've been operating that way for years and I can tell you, it's made my life miserable as hell!

Well-being is available to us in every moment, provided that we know how to look for it. Positive states of the mind are precious skills that can be learned, and for the most part, it's just a question of habit.

For example, get into the habit of seeing the positive in every circumstance. I promise you, even the worst case scenarios have something positive attached to them. Also, when you're doing something you're passionate about (and I hope it's trading), whatever happens to you and whatever you decide is worthy of your time, heart, and focus. So rest as this condition. You're doing what you love. And that is happiness.

Recalibrate your behavior, every day

Every day, we rise up, as if born again. So every day we have this potential to reinvent ourselves, and start fresh. And this means that every day we could learn to reformulate our intentions, recalibrate our behaviors, get out of bad habits, and thus move closer towards something that really matters to us. And that is really a gift.

Unfortunately, we're so used to this passing of days that we don't really see it as an opportunity. For us, one day leads to the other, and the other, and the other. It seems like a never ending cycle so our mind automatically thinks that it has time to do those things later.

But there is an illusion here that we're not seeing. As days pass, we are slowly moving towards our death.

My friends, don't let death, in the end, remind you how insubstantial your worries, anxieties, self-doubts, and self-criticisms were. Time is a precious asset. Don't let it slip through your hands without having achieved anything worthwhile. Act now! You already have everything in you to be what you want to be and to do what you want to do.

NOTES AND REFERENCES

In chapter 3, I talk about how our primitive mind is often pitted against our more rational mind. This is the research that points to it

https://www.psychologytoday.com/files/attachments/51483/handling-the-hijack.pdf

----

In chapter 4, I briefly touch on the only fear (of falling) that is passed on to us via our genes. This is the research that supports this view:

http://www.parents.com/baby/development/behavioral/emotions-in-the-first-year/

The following two books helped me deepen my understanding of the brain and its functions. These books are exceptionally well written and contain mostly scientific information and thoughtful analysis.

The Brain That Changes Itself: Stories of Personal Triumph from the Frontiers of Brain Science by Norman Doidge

http://www.amazon.com/gp/product/0143113100/ref=as_li_ss_tl?ie=UTF8&keywords=the%20brain%20that%20changes%20itself&qid=1457301685&ref_=sr_1_1&sr=8-1&linkCode=sl1&tag=wwwtradingcom-20&linkId=5bab0c30d1ab3ca695b77addf17bc24d

Incognito: The Secret Lives of the Brain by David Eagleman

Once and for all, over the last decades, scientific research has proven the benefits of meditation/ mindfulness (no difference between the two, just semantics).

Here's a non-exaustive list of that research:

1. Meditation reduces the "monkey mind"

One of the most interesting studies in the last few years, carried out at Yale University, found that mindfulness meditation decreases activity in the default mode network-the brain network responsible for mind-wandering and self-referential thoughts. The default mode network (DMN) is active when we are not focusing on anything in particular; when our minds are just wandering from thought to thought, like a monkey jumping from branch to branch.

This is where the Buddhist expression "Monkey mind" comes from – it refers to the incessant chatter that goes on in our heads. Since mind-wandering is typically associated with being less happy, ruminating, and worrying about the past and future, it is the "goal" of meditation to dial it down. And several studies have shown that meditation, through its quieting effect on the DMN, appears to do just this.

Eventually, when the mind does start to wander like it just naturally does (and always will do), because of the new connections that form, meditators are better at snapping back out of it.

This is particularly significant for us traders as it allows us to reroute our attention to the present whenever we catch ourselves indulging in thoughts of past or future trades; wins or losses, or any kind of weighing, judging, or doubting. The ability to stay presently focused on the now moment allows us to trade and manage our current positions to the best of our abilities. It allows us to see market action from an objective and impartial stand point.

http://www.pnas.org/content/108/50/20254.short

2. It decreases depression

Do you feel depressed when you lose in the markets? Do you tend to ruminate on why the markets didn't accommodate you? A study conducted in Belgium, involving a decent sample of 400 students (age 13 - 20), concluded that participants who followed an in-class mindfulness program reported a reduction in depression, anxiety, and stress. Moreover, these students were less likely to develop pronounced depression-like symptoms.

Another study, from the University of California, concluded that mindfulness meditation decreases ruminative thinking and dysfunctional beliefs in people who struggled with depression in the past.

Yet another concludes that mindfulness meditation may be effective to treat depression to a similar degree as antidepressant drug therapy.

3. It reduces stress and anxiety

A study from the University of Wisconsin-Madison indicates that the practice of Meditation reduces the grey-matter density in areas of the brain related with anxiety and stress. The individuals who participated in the study were more able to attend moment-to-moment to the stream of stimuli to which they were exposed and less likely to 'get stuck' on any one stimulus. In other words, when we monitor non-reactively the contents of experience, furthermore the contents of consciousness, from moment-to-moment primarily as a means to recognize the nature of emotional and cognitive patterns, but also as a mean to better understand some fundamental truths about the nature of the environment that surrounds us, we reduce the apprehension of future events. Along the way, we reduce stress and anxiety!

4. It helps reduce symptoms of panic disorder

In a research published in the American Journal of Psychiatry, 22 patients diagnosed with anxiety or panic disorders were submitted to a 3 months meditation and relaxation training. As a result, for 20 of those patients the effects of panic and anxiety had reduced substantially, and the changes were maintained at follow-up.

http://ajp.psychiatryonline.org/doi/abs/10.1176/ajp.149.7.936

5. It increases grey matter concentration in the brain

A group of Harvard neuroscientists ran an experiment where 16 people were submitted to an eight-week mindfulness course, using guided meditations and integration of mindfulness into everyday activities. At the end of it, MRI scans showed that the grey matter concentration increased in areas of the brain involved in learning and memory, but also regulating emotions, sense of self, and having perspective. In other words, if we cultivate a regular practice, our perspective on life's circumstances and experience becomes more faithful to the way things really are.

http://www.psyn-journal.com/article/S0925-4927%2810%2900288-X/abstract
http://www.sciencedirect.com/science/article/pii/S1051053811909000

6. It improves your focus, attention, and ability to work under stress

A study led by The University of California suggested that during and after a meditation training, subjects were more skilled at keeping focus, especially on repetitive and boring tasks.

Another study demonstrated that even with only 20 minutes a day of practice, students were able to improve their performance on tests involving cognitive skill, in some cases doing 10 times better than another group that did not meditate. They also performed better on information-processing tasks that were designed to induce deadline stress.

In fact, there is evidence that meditators have thicker prefrontal cortex and right anterior insula, and to this effect the practice might offset the loss of cognitive abilities associated with old age.

http://content.time.com/time/health/article/0,8599,2008914,00.html
http://link.springer.com/article/10.3758/CABN.7.2.109#page-1

7. It improves information processing and decision-making

A study done at the UCLA Laboratory of Neuro Imaging suggest that long-term meditators have larger amounts of gyrification ("folding" of the cortex, which may allow the brain to process information faster) than people who do not meditate. Scientists suspect that gyrification is responsible for making the brain better at processing information, making decisions, forming memories and improving attention.

http://newsroom.ucla.edu/releases/evidence-builds-that-meditation-230237

8. It gives you mental strength, resilience and emotional intelligence

PhD psychotherapist Dr. Ron Alexander reports in his book Wise Mind, Open Mind that the process of controlling the mind, through meditation, increases mental strength, resilience, and emotional intelligence.

9. It increases your ability to keep focus in spite of distractions

A study from Emory University, Atlanta, demonstrated that participants with more meditation experience exhibit increased connectivity within the brain networks controlling attention. These neural relationships may be involved in the development of cognitive skills, such as maintaining attention and disengaging from distraction.

Moreover, the benefits of the practice were observed also in normal state of consciousness during the day, which speaks to the transference of cognitive abilities "off the cushion" into daily life.

BONUS

My gift to you

Thank you for reading this book. I hope I was successful in reflecting back to you some things that maybe were out of your perspective. As insightful or revealing as those things were, I have to admit, it's difficult to change deep mental conditionings and patterns of behavior through the sheer reading of a book. You have to take action!

I have designed a course called *The Trading Psychology Mastery Course* to help you with that, and I can tell you, it is unlike anything you've seen! In it, I aspire to help you develop into an emotionally intelligent trader, regardless of your background. I am a trader with several years of experience in anything pertaining to meditation and present moment awareness. I don't just talk the talk, I walk it, extensively. I've been to countless extended retreats, studied with many renowned "enlightened" teachers and gurus, and I have developed a thorough understanding of my mind.

Meditation/ Mindfulness have provoked some deep transformational changes in me and the way I trade, and in the course, I help traders go through that same process of transformation.

The implications of such profound mental changes are enormous for us traders. When equanimity, balance, wise discernment, among other wholesome mental characteristics become the new norm of the mind, what ensues is a way of trading that is effortless, enjoyable, and above all profitable!

So, I know how to guide you through your journey, and I can tell you, you have all to gain and nothing to lose. Well... the only thing you stand to lose is your ego... but that's a good thing, trust me.

If you like this book (or any of my other books); in my course, we work on developing an experiential understanding of everything that has been discussed in the books, but there are some new stuff as well.

Market success begins with stability of mind, flexibility, concentration, and non-attachment, all of which are explored in detail in this two-week practical and deep home immersion. In it you will learn:

• How you create your own results in the

markets – good or bad.

- To work with obstacles, such as our mental conditioning, or our normal propensity for not accepting risk; for wanting to be right, craving certain, and so on.

- To detach yourself from the concept of money for a smoother trading experience

- How to deepen your concentration, and focus

- Self-regulation, so no matter what the markets do and no matter what they throw at you, you'll remain equanimous and unperturbed.

- And more…

The following is required of you, if you decide to enroll in the course:

- Get yourself a journal

- Abstinence from any trading activity for 2 weeks

- Commitment, commitment, commitment!

Very few traders work on developing strong skills of introspection. I know absolutely brilliant people who could have been extraordinary traders if they had cultivated an ability to make the most basic discrimination about their moment to moment experience.

Conversely, I've met many traders who aren't especially brilliant but who are so in tune with themselves that they are unshakable and equanimous in the midst of uncertainty and vicissitudes, and this makes all the difference, in terms of their trading results.

So, if you can commit to this course wholehearted, you will begin to gain insight into the way you live and think. You will see how it is affecting your trading results. You will see how you are seeing the markets through your own set of filters, and not for what it truly is.

The barriers we face in our trading are always a function of the stories we tell ourselves. You will learn to calm your mind and to drop beneath the stories. You will begin to experience your trading in a whole new way. Sometimes shifts are dramatic and sometimes gradual, but I will guide you and support you through this whole journey, and you should start seeing results within a month. Yes, one month!

So, enroll if:

• You think you might be up for the challenge (and promise you, it's going to be a challenge!).

- If you want to learn more about yourself. By 'conquering' yourself, you will conquer the markets

- If you are serious about your trading career (and your life)

The course is priced at 200 USD, but if you use the code below, you get 50 USD off that price. That's my gift to you! And I want to inform you that the price tag of 200 dollars is likely to increase in the future as I continue to make improvements to the program. So this is your chance to lock in a lifetime access to the program – $50 off!

I hope to see you in!

Head to www.tradingcomposure.com
Enter this coupon code: <u>EQUANIMITY</u>

<u>Important:</u> When you come to the payment page there is a very faint option under the USD 200 box (you have to place your cursor on it to see it). When you click on it, you will be asked to input any coupon you have.

CAN I ASK A FAVOUR?

I would really appreciate it if you would post a short review of this book on amazon. Good or bad, just make it honest to help others in their choice.

Also, it takes time to write these books and I do read all the reviews personally. That way I can continually write what people are wanting. So, I really value your support in that project.

Made in the USA
Monee, IL
01 December 2020